Pandora's Box: A Tragedy In Three Acts

Frank Wedekind, Samuel Atkins Eliot

PANDORA'S BOX

A TRAGEDY IN THREE ACTS

BY

FRANK WEDEKIND

Translated by Samuel A. Eliot, Jr.

BONI AND LIVERIGHT
NEW YORK 1918

PANDORA'S BOX

CHARACTERS

LULU.
ALVA SCHÖN, *writer.*
SCHIGOLCH.
RODRIGO QUAST, *acrobat.*
ALFRED HUGENBERG, *escaped from a reform-school.*
COUNTESS GESCHWITZ.

BIANETTA. LUDMILLA STEINHERZ. MAGELONE. KADIDIA, *her daughter.* COUNT CASTI PIANI. PUNTSCHU, *a banker.* HEILMANN, *a journalist.* BOB, *a groom.* A DETECTIVE.	In Act II.
MR. HUNIDEI. KUNGU POTI, *imperial prince of Uahubee.* DR. HILTI, *tutor.* JACK.	In Act I

ACT I

The hall of EARTH-SPIRIT, Act IV, *feebly lighted by an oil lamp on the centre table. Even this is dimmed by a heavy shade. Lulu's picture is gone from the easel, which still stands by the foot of the stairs. The fire-screen and the chair by the ottoman are gone too. Down left is a small tea-table, with a coffee-pot and a cup of black coffee on it, and an arm-chair next it.*

In this chair, deep in cushions, with a plaid shawl over her knees, sits Countess Geschwitz in a tight black dress. Rodrigo, clad as a servant, sits on the ottoman. At the rear, Alva Schön is walking up and down before the entrance door.

RODRIGO. He lets people wait for him as if he were a concert conductor!

GESCHWITZ. I beg of you, don't speak!

RODRIGO. Hold my tongue, with a head as full of thoughts as mine is!—I absolutely can't believe she's changed so awfully much to her advantage there!

GESCHWITZ. She is more glorious to look at than I have ever seen her!

RODRIGO. God preserve me from founding my life-happiness on your taste and judgment! If the sickness has hit her as it has you, I'm smashed and thru! You're leaving the contagious ward like an acrobat-lady who's had an accident after giving herself up to art. You can scarcely blow your nose any more. First you need a quarter-hour to sort your fingers, and then you have to be mighty careful not to break off the tip.

GESCHWITZ. What puts us under the ground gives her health and strength again.

RODRIGO. That's all right and fine enough. But I don't think I'll be travelling off with her this evening.

GESCHWITZ. You will let your bride journey all alone, after all?

RODRIGO. In the first place, the old fellow's going with her to protect her in case anything serious—. My escort could only be suspicious. And secondly, I must wait here till my costumes are ready. I'll get across the frontier soon enough alright,—and I hope in the meantime she'll put on a little embonpoint, too. Then we'll get married, provided I can present her before a respectable public. I love the practical in a woman: what theories they make up for themselves are all the same to me. Aren't they to you too, doctor?

ALVA. I haven't heard what you were saying.

RODRIGO. I'd never have got my person mixed up in this plot if she hadn't kept tickling my bare pate, before her sentence. If only she doesn't start doing too much as soon as she's out of Germany! I'd like best to take her to London for six months, and let her fill up on plum-cakes. In London one expands just from the sea air. And then, too, in London one doesn't feel with every swallow of beer as if the hand of fate were at one's throat.

ALVA. I've been asking myself for a week whether a person who'd been sentenced to prison could still be made to go as the chief figure in a modern drama.

GESCHWITZ. If the man would only come, now!

RODRIGO. I've still got to redeem my properties out of the pawn-shop here, too. Six hundred kilos of the best iron. The baggage-rate on 'em is always three times as much as my own ticket, so that the whole junket isn't worth a trowser's button. When I went into the pawn-shop with 'em, dripping with sweat, they asked me if the things were genuine!—I'd have really done better to have had the costumes made abroad. In Paris, for instance, they see at the first glance where one's best points are, and bravely lay them bare. But you can't learn that with bow-legs; it's got to be studied on classically shaped people. In this country they're as scared of naked skin as they are abroad of dynamite bombs. A couple of years ago I was fined fifty marks at the Alhambra Theater, because people could see I had a few hairs on my chest, not enough to make a respectable tooth-brush! But the Fine Arts Minister opined that the little school-girls might lose their joy in knitting stockings because of it; and since then I have myself shaved once a month.

ALVA. If I didn't need every bit of my creative power now for the "World-conqueror," I might like to test the problem and see what could be done with it. That's the curse of our young literature: we're so much too literary. We know only such questions and problems as come up among writers and cultured people. We cannot see beyond the limits of our own professional interests. In order to get back on the trail of a great and powerful art we must move as much as possible among men who've never read a book in their lives, whom the simplest animal instincts direct in all they do. I've tried already, with all my might, to work according to those principles—in my "Earth-spirit." The woman who was my model for the chief figure in that, breathes to-day—and has for a year—behind barred windows; and on that account for some incomprehensible reason the play was only brought to performance by the Society for Free Literature. As long as my father was alive, all the stages of Germany stood open to my creations. That has been vastly changed.

RODRIGO. I've had a pair of tights made of the tenderest blue-green. If t h e y don't make a success abroad, I'll sell mouse-traps! The trunks are so delicate I can't sit on the edge of a table in 'em. The only thing that will disturb the good impression is my awful bald head, which I owe to my active participation in this great conspiracy. To lie in the hospital in perfect health for three months would make a fat pig of the most run-down old hobo. Since coming out I've fed on nothing but Karlsbad pills. Day and night I have orchestra rehearsals in my intestines. I'll be so washed out before I get across the frontier that I won't be able to lift a bottle-cork.

GESCHWITZ. How the attendants in the hospital got out of her way yesterday! That was a refreshing sight. The garden was still as the grave: in the loveliest noon sunlight the convalescents didn't venture out of doors. Away back by the contagious ward she stepped out under the mulberry trees and swayed on her ankles on the gravel. The door-keeper had recognized me, and a young doctor who met me in the corridor shrunk up as tho a revolver shot had struck him. The Sisters vanished into the big rooms or stayed stuck against the walls. When I came back there was not a soul to be seen in the garden or at the gate. No better chance could have been found, if we had had the cursèd passports. And now the fellow says he isn't going with her!

RODRIGO. I understand the poor hospital-brothers. One has a bad foot and another has a swollen cheek, and there appears in the midst of them the incarnate death-insurance-agentess! In the Hall of the Knights, as the blessed division was called from which I organized my spying, when the news got around there that Sister Theophila had departed this life, not one of the fellows could be kept in bed. They scrambled up to the window-bars, if they had to drag their pains along with them by the hundred-weight. I never heard such swearing in my life!

ALVA. Allow me, Fräulein von Geschwitz, to come back to my proposition once more. Tho my father was shot in this room, still I can see in the murder, as in the punishment, nothing but a horrible misfortune that has befallen h e r; nor do I think that my father, if he had come through alive, would have withdrawn his support from her entirely. Whether your plan for freeing her will succeed still seems to me very doubtful, tho I wouldn't like to discourage you; but I can find no words to express the admiration with which your self-sacrifice, your energy, your superhuman scorn of death, inspires me. I don't believe any man ever risked so much for a woman, let alone for a friend. I am not aware, Fräulein von Geschwitz, how rich you are, but the expenses for what you have accomplished must have exhausted your fortune. May I venture to offer you a loan of 20,000 marks—which I should have no trouble raising for you in cash?

GESCHWITZ. How we did rejoice when Sister Theophila was really dead! From that day on we were free from custody. We changed our beds as we liked. I had done my hair like hers, and copied every tone of her voice. When the professor came he called h e r "gnädiges Fräulein" and said to me, "It's better living here than in prison!" . . . When the Sister suddenly was missing, we looked at each other in suspense: we had both been sick five days: now was the deciding moment. Next morning came the assistant.—"How is Sister Theophila?" —"Dead!"—We communicated behind his back, and when he had gone we sank in each other's arms: "God be thanked! Gc⅃ be thanked!"—What pains it cost me to keep my darling from betraying how well she already was! "You have nine years of prison before you," I cried to her early and late. Now they probably won't let her stay in the contagious ward three days more!

RODRIGO. I lay in the hospital full three months to spy out the ground, after toilfully peddling together the qualities necessary for such a long stay. Now I act the valet here with you, Dr. Schön, so that no strange servants may come into the house. Where is the bridegroom who's ever done so much for his bride? M y fortune has also been destroyed.

ALVA. When you succeed in developing her into a respectable artiste you will have put the world in debt to you. With the temperament and the beauty that she has to give out of the depths of her nature she can make the most blasé public hold its breath. And then, too, she will be protected by a c t i n g passion from a second time becoming a criminal in reality.

RODRIGO. I'll soon drive her kiddishness out of her!

GESCHWITZ. There he comes! (*Steps louden in the gallery. Then the curtains part at the head of the stairs and Schigolch in a long black coat with a white sun-shade in his right hand comes down. Thruout the play his speech is interrupted with frequent yawns.*)

SCHIGOLCH. Confound the darkness! Out-doors the sun burns your eyes out.

GESCHWITZ. (*Wearily unwrapping herself.*) I'm coming!

RODRIGO. Her ladyship has seen no daylight for three days. We live here like in a snuff-box.

SCHIGOLCH. Since nine o'clock this morning I've been round to all the old-clothes-men. Three brand new trunks stuffed full of old trowsers I've expressed to Buenos Ayres via Bremerhaven. My legs are dangling on me like the tongue of a bell. That's the new life it's going to be from now on!

RODRIGO. Where are you going to get off to-morrow morning?

SCHIGOLCH. I hope not straight into Ox-butter Hotel again!

RODRIGO. I can tell you a fine hotel. I lived there with a lady lion-tamer. The people were born in Berlin.

GESCHWITZ. (*Upright in the arm-chair.*) Come and help me!

RODRIGO. (*Hurries to her and supports her.*) And you'll be safer from the police there than on a high tight-rope!

GESCHWITZ. He means to let you go with her alone this afternoon.

SCHIGOLCH. Maybe he's still suffering from his chill-blains!

RODRIGO. Do you want me to start my new engagement in bath-robe and slippers?

SCHIGOLCH. Hm—Sister Theophila wouldn't have gone to heaven so promptly either, if she hadn't felt so affectionate towards our patient.

RODRIGO. She'll have a different value when one must serve thru a honeymoon with her. Anyway, it can't hurt her if she gets a little fresh air beforehand.

ALVA. (*A pocketbook in his hand, to Geschwitz who*

is leaning on a chair-back by the centre table.) This holds 10,000 marks.

GESCHWITZ. Thank you, no.

ALVA. Please take it.

GESCHWITZ. (*To Schigolch.*) Come along, at last!

SCHIGOLCH. Patience, Fräulein. It's only a stone's throw across Hospital Street. I'll be here with her in five minutes.

ALVA. You're bringing her here?

SCHIGOLCH. I'm bringing her here. Or do you fear for your health?

ALVA. You see that I fear nothing.

RODRIGO. According to the latest wire, the doctor is on his way to Constantinople to have his "Earth-spirit" produced before the Sultan by harem-ladies and eunuchs.

ALVA. (*Opening the centre door under the gallery.*) It's shorter for you thru here. (*Exeunt Schigolch and Countess Geschwitz. Alva locks the door.*)

RODRIGO. You were going to give more money to the crazy sky-rocket!

ALVA. What has that to do with you?

RODRIGO. I get paid like a lamp-lighter, tho I had to demoralize all the Sisters in the hospital. Then came the assistants' and the doctors' turn, and then—

ALVA. Will you seriously inform me that the medical professors let themselves be influenced by you?

RODRIGO. With the money those gentlemen cost me I could become President of the United States!

ALVA. But Fräulein von Geschwitz has reimbursed you for every penny that you spent. So far as I know you're getting a monthly salary of five hundred marks from her besides. It is often pretty hard to believe in your love for the unhappy murderess. When I asked

Fäulein von Geschwitz just now to accept my help, it certainly was not to incite your insatiable avarice. The admiration which I have learnt to have for Fräulein von Geschwitz in this affair, I am far from feeling towards you. It is not at all clear to me what claims of any kind you can make upon me. That you chanced to be present at the murder of my father has not yet created the slightest bond of relationship between you and me. On the contrary, I am firmly convinced that if the heroic undertaking of Countess Geschwitz had not come your way you would be lying somewhere to-day without a penny, drunken in the gutter.

RODRIGO. And do you know what would have become of you if you hadn't sold for two millions the tuppeny paper your father ran? You'd have hitched up with the stringiest sort of ballet-girl and been to-day a stable-boy in the Humpelmeier Circus. What work do you do? You've written a drama of horrors in which my bride's calves are the two chief figures and which no high-class theater will produce. You walking pajamas! You fresh rag-bag you! Two years ago I balanced two saddled cavalry-horses on this chest. How that'll go now, after this (*clasping his bald head*), is a question sure enough. The foreign girls will get a fine idea of German art when they see the sweat come beading thru my tights at every fresh kilo-weight! I shall make the whole auditorium stink with my exhalations!

ALVA. You're weak as a dish-clout!

RODRIGO. Would to God you were right! or did you perhaps intend to insult me? If so, I'll set the tip of my toe to your jaw so that your tongue'll crawl along the carpet over there!

ALVA. Try it! (*Steps and voices outside.*) Who is that . . .?

RODRIGO. You can thank God that I have no public here before me!

ALVA. Who can that be!

RODRIGO. That is my beloved. It's a full year now since we've seen each other.

ALVA. But how should they be back already! Who can be coming there? I expect no one.

RODRIGO. Oh the devil, unlock it!

ALVA. Hide yourself!

RODRIGO. I'll get behind the portières. I've stood there once before, a year ago. (*Disappears, right. Alva opens the rear door, whereupon Alfred Hugenberg enters, hat in hand.*)

ALVA. With whom have I— . . . You? Aren't you—?

HUGENBERG. Alfred Hugenberg.

ALVA. What can I do for you?

HUGENBERG. I've come from Münsterburg. I ran away this morning.

ALVA. My eyes are bad. I am forced to keep the blinds closed.

HUGENBERG. I need your help. You will not refuse me. I've got a plan ready. Can anyone hear us?

ALVA. What do you mean? What sort of a plan?

HUGENBERG. Are you alone?

ALVA. Yes. What do you want to impart to me?

HUGENBERG. I've had two plans already that I let drop. What I shall tell you now has been worked out to the last possible chance. If I had money I should not confide it to you; I thought about that a long time before coming . . . Will you not permit me to set forth to you my design?

ALVA. Will you kindly tell me just what you are talking about?

HUGENBERG. She cannot possibly be so indifferent to you that I must tell you that. The evidence *you* gave the coroner helped her more than everything the defending counsel said.

ALVA. I beg to decline the supposition.

HUGENBERG. You would say that; I understand that, of course. But all the same you were her best witness.

ALVA. *You* were! You said my father was about to force her to shoot herself.

HUGENBERG. He was, too. But they didn't believe me. I wasn't put on my oath.

ALVA. Where have you come from now?

HUGENBERG. From a reform-school I broke out of this morning.

ALVA. And what do you have in view?

HUGENBERG. I'm trying to get into the confidence of a turnkey.

ALVA. What do you mean to live on?

HUGENBERG. I'm living with a girl who's had a child by my father.

ALVA. Who is your father?

HUGENBERG. He's a police captain. I know the prison without ever having been inside it; and nobody in it will recognize me as I am now. But I don't count on that at all. I know an iron ladder by which one can get from the first court to the roof and thru an opening there into the attic. There's no way up to it from inside. But in all five wings boards and laths and great heaps of shavings are lying under the roofs, and I'll drag them all together in the middle and set fire to them. My pockets are full of matches and all the things used to make fires.

ALVA. But then you'll burn up there!

HUGENBERG. Of course, if I'm not rescued. But to get into the first court I must have the turnkey in my power, and for that I need money. Not that I mean to bribe him; that wouldn't go. I must lend him money to send his three children to the country, and then at four o'clock in the morning when the prisoners of respected families are discharged, I'll slip in the door. He'll lock-up behind me and ask me what I'm after, and I'll ask him to let me out again in the evening. And before it gets light, I'm up in the attic.

ALVA. How did you escape from the reform-school?

HUGENBERG. Jumped out the window. I need two hundred marks for the rascal to send his family to the country.

RODRIGO. (*Stepping out of the portières, right.*) Will the Herr Baron have coffee in the music-room or on the veranda?

HUGENBERG. Where does that man come from? Out of the same door! He jumped out of the same door!

ALVA. I've taken him into my service. He is dependable.

HUGENBERG. (*Grasping his temples.*) Fool that I am! Oh, fool!

RODRIGO. Oh, yah, we've seen each other here before! Cut away now to your vice-mamma. Your kid brother might like to uncle his brothers and sisters. Make your sir-papa the grandfather of his children! You're the only thing we've missed. If you once get into my sight in the next two weeks, I'll beat your bean up for porridge.

ALVA. Be quiet, you!

HUGENBERG. I'm a fool!

RODRIGO. What do you want to do with your fire? Don't you know the lady's been dead three weeks?

HUGENBERG. Did they cut off her head?

RODRIGO. No, she's got that still. She was mashed by the cholera.

HUGENBERG. That is not true!

RODRIGO. What do you know about it! There, read it: here! (*Taking out a paper and pointing to the place.*) "The murderess of Dr. Schön . . ." (*Gives Hugenberg the paper. He reads:*)

HUGENBERG. "The murderess of Dr. Schön has in some incomprehensible way fallen ill of the cholera in prison." It doesn't say that she's dead.

RODRIGO. Well, what else do you suppose she is? She's been lying in the churchyard three weeks. Back in the left-hand corner behind the rubbish-heap where the little crosses are with no names on them, there she lies under the first one. You'll know the spot because the grass hasn't grown on it. Hang a tin wreath there, and then get back to your nursery-school or I'll denounce you to the police. I know the female that beguiles her leisure hours with you!

HUGENBERG. (*To Alva.*) Is it true that she's dead?

ALVA. Thank God, yes!—Please, do not keep me here any longer. My doctor has forbidden me to receive visitors.

HUGENBERG. My future is worth so little now! I would gladly have given the last scrap of what life is worth to me for her happiness. Heigh-ho! One way or another I'll sure go to the devil now!

RODRIGO. If you dare in any way to approach me or the doctor here or my honorable friend Schigolch too near, I'll inform on you for intended arson. You need three good years, to learn where not to stick your fingers in! Now get out!

HUGENBERG. Fool!

RODRIGO. Get out!! (*Throws him out the door. Coming down.*) I wonder you didn't put your purse at that rogue's disposal, too!

ALVA. I won't stand your damned jabbering! The boy's little finger is worth more than all you!

RODRIGO. I've had enough of this Geschwitz's company! If my bride is to become a corporation with limited liability, somebody else can go in ahead of me. I propose to make a magnificent trapeze-artist out of her, and willingly risk my life to do it. But then I'll be master of the house, and will myself indicate what cavaliers she is to receive!

ALVA. The boy has what our age lacks: a hero-nature; therefore, of course, he is going to ruin. Do you remember how before sentence was passed he jumped out of the witness-box and yelled at the justice: "How do you know what would have become of you if you'd had to run around the cafés barefoot every night when you were ten years old?!"

RODRIGO. If I could only have given him one in the jaw for that right away! Thank God, there are jails where scum like that gets some respect for the law pounded into them.

ALVA. One like him might have been my model for my "World-conqueror." For twenty years literature has presented nothing but demi-men: men who can beget no children and women who can bear none. That's called "The Modern Problem."

RODRIGO. I've ordered a hippopotamus-whip two inches thick. If that has no success with her, you can fill my cranium with potato-soup. Be it love or be it whipping, female flesh never inquires. Only give it some amusement, and it stays firm and fresh. She is now in her twentieth year, has been married three times and has satisfied a gigantic horde of lovers, and her heart's desires are at last pretty plain. But the man's got to have the seven deadly sins on his forehead, or she honors him not. If he looks as if a dog-catcher had spat him out on the street, then, with such women-folks, he needn't be afraid of a prince! I'll rent a garage fifty feet high and break her in there; and when she's learnt the first diving-leap without breaking her neck I'll pull on a black coat and not stir a finger the rest of my life. When she's educated practically it doesn't cost a woman half as much trouble to support her husband as the other way round, if only the man takes care of the mental labor for her, and doesn't let the sense of the family go to wreck.

ALVA. I have learnt to rule humanity and drive it in harness before me like a well-broken four-in-hand,—but that boy sticks in my head. Really, I can still take private lessons in the scorn of the world from that school-boy!

RODRIGO. She'll just comfortably let her hide be papered with thousand-mark bills! I'll extract salaries out of the directors with a centrifugal pump. I know their kind. When they don't need a man, let him shine their shoes for them; but when they must have an artiste they cut her down from the very gallows with their own hands and with the most entangling compliments.

ALVA. In my situation there's nothing more in the world to fear—but death. In the realm of sensation I am the poorest beggar. But I can no longer scrape up the moral courage to exchange my established position for the excitements of the wild, adventurous life!

RODRIGO. She had sent Papa Schigolch and me together in chase of some strong antidote for sleeplessness. We each got a twenty-mark piece for expenses. There we see the youngster sitting in the Night-light Café. He was sitting like a criminal on the prisoner's bench. Schigolch sniffed at him from all sides, and remarked, "He is still virgin." (*Up in the gallery, dragging steps are heard.*) There she is! The future magnificent trapeze-artiste of the present age!

(*The curtains part at the stair-head, and Lulu, supported by Schigolch, and in a black dress, slowly and wearily descends.*)

SCHIGOLCH. Hui, old mold! We've still to get over the frontier to-day.

RODRIGO. (*Glaring stupidly at Lulu.*) Thunder of heaven! Death!

LULU. (*Speaks, to the end of the act, in the gayest tones.*) Slowly! You're pinching my arm!

RODRIGO. How did you ever get the shamelessness to break out of prison with such a wolf's face?!

SCHIGOLCH. Stop your snout!

RODRIGO. I'll run for the police! I'll give information! This scarecrow let herself be seen in tights?! The padding alone would cost two months' salary!—You're the most perfidious swindler that ever had lodging in Ox-butter Hotel!

ALVA. Kindly refrain from insulting the lady!

RODRIGO. Insulting you call that?! For this gnawed

bone's sake I've worn myself away! I can't earn my own living! I'll be a clown if I can still stand firm under a broom-stick! But let the lightning strike me on the spot if I don't worm ten thousand marks a year for life out of your tricks and frauds! I can tell you that! A pleasant trip! I'm going for the police! (*Exit.*)

SCHIGOLCH. Run, run!

LULU. He'll take good care of himself!

SCHIGOLCH. We're rid of h i m!—And now some black coffee for the lady!

ALVA. (*At the table left.*) Here is coffee, ready to pour.

SCHIGOLCH. I must look after the sleeping-car tickets.

LULU. (*Brightly.*) Oh, freedom! Thank God for freedom!

SCHIGOLCH. I'll be back for you in half an hour. We'll celebrate our departure in the station-restaurant. I'll order a supper that'll keep us going till to-morrow.—Good morning, doctor.

ALVA. Good evening.

SCHIGOLCH. Pleasant rest!—Thanks, I know every door-handle here. So long! Have a good time! (*Exit.*)

LULU. I haven't seen a room for a year and a half. Curtains, chairs, pictures . . .

ALVA. Won't you drink it?

LULU. I've swallowed enough black coffee these five days. Have you any brandy?

ALVA. I've got some elixir de Spaa.

LULU. That reminds one of old times. (*Looks round the hall while Alva fills two glasses.*) Where's my picture gone?

ALVA. I've got it in my room, so no one shall see it here.

LULU. Bring it down here now.

ALVA. Didn't you even lose your vanity in prison?

LULU. How anxious at heart one gets when one hasn't seen herself for months! One day I got a brand-new dust-pan. When I swept up at seven in the morning I held the back of it up before my face. Tin doesn't flatter, but I took pleasure in it all the same.—Bring the picture down from your room. Shall I come too?

ALVA. No, Heaven's sake! You must spare yourself!

LULU. I've been sparing myself long enough now! (*Alva goes out, right, to get the picture.*) He has heart-trouble; but to have to plague one's self with imagination fourteen months! . . . He kisses with the fear of death on him, and his two knees shake like a frozen vagabond's. In God's name . . . In this room—if only I had not shot his father in the back!

ALVA. (*Returns with the picture of Lulu in the Pierrot-dress.*) It's covered with dust. I had leant it against the fire-place, face to the wall.

LULU. You didn't look at it all the time I was away?

ALVA. I had so much business to attend to, with the sale of our paper and everything. Countess Geschwitz would have liked to have hung it up in her house, but she had to be prepared for search-warrants. (*He puts the picture on the easel.*)

LULU. (*Merrily.*) Now the poor monster is learning the joys of life in Hotel Ox-butter by her own experience.

ALVA. Even now I don't understand how events hang together.

LULU. Oh, Geschwitz arranged it all very cleverly.

I must admire her inventiveness. But the cholera must have raged fearfully in Hamburg this summer; and on that she founded her plan for freeing me. She took a course in hospital nursing here, and when she had the necessary documents she journeyed to Hamburg with them and nursed the cholera patients. At the first opportunity that offered she put on the underclothes in which a sick woman had just died and which really ought to have been burnt. The same morning she traveled back here and came to see me in prison. In my cell, while the wardress was outside, we, as quick as we could, exchanged underclothes.

ALVA. So that was the reason why the Countess and you fell sick of the cholera the same day!

LULU. Exactly, that was it! Geschwitz of course was instantly brought from her house to the contagious ward in the hospital. But with me, too, they couldn't think of any other place to take me. So there we lay in one room in the contagious ward behind the hospital, and from the first day Geschwitz put forth all her art to make our two faces as like each other as possible. Day before yesterday she was let out as cured. Just now she came back and said she'd forgotten her watch. I put on her clothes, she slipped into my prison frock, and then I came away. (*With pleasure.*) Now she's lying over there as the murderess of Dr. Schön.

ALVA. So far as outward appearance goes you can still agree with the picture as much as ever.

LULU. I'm a little peaked in the face, but otherwise I've lost nothing. Only one gets incredibly nervous in prison.

ALVA. You looked horribly sick when you came in.

LULU. I had to, to get our necks out of the noose.—And you? What have you done in this year and a half?

ALVA. I've had a succès d'estime in literary circles with a play I wrote about you.

LULU. Who's your sweetheart now?

ALVA. An actress I've rented a house for in Karl Street.

LULU. Does she love you?

ALVA. How should I know that? I haven't seen the woman for six weeks.

LULU. Can you stand that?

ALVA. You will never understand that. With me there's the closest alternation between my sensuality and mental creativeness. So towards you, for example, I have only the choice of regarding you artistically or of loving you.

LULU. (*In a fairy-story tone.*) I used to dream every other night that I'd fallen into the hands of a sadic . . . Come, give me a kiss!

ALVA. It's shining in your eyes like the water in a deep well one has just thrown a stone into.

LULU. Come!

ALVA. (*Kisses her.*) Your lips have got pretty thin, anyway.

LULU. Come! (*Pushes him into a chair and seats herself on his knee.*) Do you shudder at me?—In Hotel Ox-butter we all got a luke-warm bath every four weeks. The wardresses took that opportunity to search our pockets as soon as we were in the water. (*She kisses him passionately.*)

ALVA. Oh, oh!

LULU. You're afraid that when I'm away you couldn't write any more poems about me?

ALVA. On the contrary, I shall write a dithyramb upon thy glory.

LULU. I'm only sore about the hideous shoes I'm wearing.

ALVA. They do not encroach upon your charms. Let us be thankful for the favor of this moment.

LULU. I don't feel at all like that to-day.—Do you remember the costume ball where I was dressed like a knight's squire? How those wine-full women ran after me that time? Geschwitz crawled round, round my feet, and begged me to step on her face with my cloth shoes.

ALVA. Come, dear heart!

LULU. (*In the tone with which one quiets a restless child.*) Quietly! I shot your father.

ALVA. I do not love thee less for that. One kiss!

LULU. Bend your head back. (*She kisses him with deliberation.*)

ALVA. You hold back the fire of my soul with the most dexterous art. And your breast breathes so virginly too. Yet if it weren't for your two great, dark, childish eyes, I must needs have thought you the cunningest whore that ever hurled a man to destruction.

LULU. (*In high spirits.*) Would God I were! Come over the border with us to-day! Then we can see each other as often as we will, and we'll get more pleasure from each other than now.

ALVA. Through this dress I feel your body like a symphony. These slender ankles, this cantabile. This rapturous crescendo. And these knees, this capriccio. And the powerful andante of lust!—How peacefully these two slim rivals press against each other in the consciousness that neither equals the other in beauty—till their capricious mistress wakes up and the rival lovers separate like the two hostile poles. I shall sing your praises so that your senses shall whirl!

LULU. (*Merrily.*) Meanwhile I'll bury my hands in your hair. (*She does so.*) But here we'll be disturbed.

ALVA. You have robbed me of my reason!

LULU. Aren't you coming with me to-day?

ALVA. But the old fellow's going with you!

LULU. He won't turn up again.—Is not that the divan on which your father bled to death?

ALVA. Be still. Be still. . . .

CURTAIN.

ACT II

A spacious salon in white stucco. In the rear-wall, between two high mirrors, a wide folding doorway showing in the rear room a big card-table surrounded by Turkish upholstered chairs. In the left wall two doors, the upper one to the entrance-hall, the lower to the dining-room. Between them a rococo-console with a white marble top, and above it Lulu's Pierrot-picture in a narrow gold frame let into the wall. Two other doors, right; near the lower one a small table. Wide and brightly-covered chairs stand about, with thin legs and fragile arms; and in the middle is a sofa of the same style (Louis XV.).

A large company is moving about the salon in lively conversation. The men—Alva, Rodrigo, Marquis Casti-Piani, Banker Puntschu, and Journalist Heilmann—are in evening dress. Lulu wears a white Directoire dress with huge sleeves and white lace falling freely from belt to feet. Her arms are in white kid gloves, her hair done high with a little tuft of white feathers. Geschwitz is in a bright blue hussar-waist trimmed with white fur and laced with silver braid, a tall tight collar with a white bow and stiff cuffs with huge ivory links. Magelone is in bright rainbow-colored shot silk with very wide sleeves, long narrow waist, and three ruffles of spiral rose-colored ribbons and violet bouquets. Her hair is parted in the middle and drawn low over her temples. On her forehead is a mother-of-pearl ornament, held by a fine chain under her hair. Kadidia, her daughter, twelve years old, has bright-green satin gaiters which yet leave visible the tops of her white silk socks, and a white-lace-covered dress with bright-green narrow sleeves, pearl-gray gloves, and free black hair under a big bright-green hat with white feathers. B i a n e t t a *is in dark-green velvet, the collar sewn with pearls, and a full skirt, its hem embroidered with great false topazes set in silver.* L u d m i l l a S t e i n h e r z *is in a glaring summer frock striped red and blue.*

Rodrigo stands, centre, a full glass in his hand.

RODRIGO. Ladies and gentlemen—I beg your pardon —please be quiet—I drink—permit me to drink—for this is the birthday party of our amiable hostess—(*taking Lulu's arm*) of Countess Adelaide d'Oubra—damned and done for!—I drink therefore — — and so forth, go to it, ladies! (*All surround Lulu and clink with her. Alva presses Rodrigo's hand.*)

ALVA. I congratulate you.

RODRIGO. I'm sweating like a roast pig.

ALVA. (*To Lulu.*) Let's see if everything's in order in the card-room. (*Alva and Lulu exeunt, rear. Bianetta speaks to Rodrigo.*)

BIANETTA. They were telling me just now you were the strongest man in the world.

RODRIGO. That I am. May I put my strength at your disposal?

MAGELONE. I love sharp-shooters better. Three months ago a sharp-shooter stepped into the casino and every time he went "bang!" I felt like this. (*She wriggles her hips.*)

CASTI-PIANI. (*Who speaks thruout the act in a bored and weary tone, to Magelone.*) Say, dearie, how does it happen we see your nice little princess here for the first time to-night? (*Meaning Kadidia.*)

MAGELONE. Do you really find her so delightful?—She is still in the convent. She must be back in school again on Monday.

KADIDIA. What did you say, mama?

MAGELONE. I was just telling the gentleman that you got the highest mark in geometry last week.

HEILMANN. Some pretty hair she's got!

CASTI-PIANI. Just look at her feet: the way she walks!

PUNTSCHU. By god, she's got breeding!

MAGELONE. (*Smiling.*) But my dear sirs, take pity on her! She's nothing but a child still!

PUNTSCHU. That'd trouble me damned little! (*To Heilmann.*) I'd give ten years of my life if I could initiate the young lady into the ceremonies of our secret society!

MAGELONE. But you won't get me to consent to that for a million. I won't have the child's youth ruined, the way mine was!

CASTI-PIANI. Confessions of a lovely soul! (*To Magelone.*) Would you not agree, either, for a set of real diamonds?

MAGELONE. Don't brag! You'll give as few real diamonds to me as to my child. You know that quite the best yourself. (*Kadidia goes into the rear room.*)

GESCHWITZ. But is nobody at all going to play, this evening?

LUDMILLA. Why, of course, comtesse. I'm counting on it very much, for one!

BIANETTA. Then let's take our places right away. The gentlemen will soon come then.

GESCHWITZ. May I ask you to excuse me just a second. I must say a word to my friend.

CASTI-PIANI. (*Offering his arm to Bianetta.*) May I have the honor to be your partner? You always hold such a lucky hand!

LUDMILLA. Now just give me your other arm and then lead us into the gambling-hell. (*The three go off so, rear.*)

MAGELONE. Say, Mr. Puntschu, have you still got a few Jungfrau shares for me, maybe?

PUNTSCHU. Jungfrau-shares? (*To Heilmann.*) The lady means the stock of the funicular railway on the Jungfrau. The Jungfrau, you know,—the Virgin—is a mountain up which they want to build a wire railway. (*To Magelone.*) You know, just so there may be no confusion;—and how easy that would be in this select circle!—Yes, I still have some four thousand Jungfrau-shares, but I should like to keep those for myself. There won't be such another chance soon of making a little fortune out of hand.

HEILMANN. I've only one lone share of this Jungfrau-stock so far. I should like to have more, too.

PUNTSCHU. I'll try, Mr. Heilmann, to look after some for you. But I'll tell you beforehand you'll have to pay drug-store prices for them!

MAGELONE. My fortune-teller advised me to look about me in time. All my savings are in Jungfrau-shares now. If it doesn't turn out well, Mr. Puntschu, I'll scratch your eyes out!

PUNTSCHU. I am perfectly sure of my affairs, my dearie!

ALVA. (*Who has come back from the card-room, to Magelone.*) I can guarantee your fears are absolutely unfounded. I paid very dear for my Jungfrau-stock and haven't regretted it a minute. They're going up steadily from day to day. There never was such a thing before.

MAGELONE. All the better, if you're right. (*Taking Puntschu's arm.*) Come, my friend, let's try our luck now at baccarat. (*All go out, rear, except Geschwitz and Rodrigo who scribbles something on a piece of paper and folds it up, then notices Geschwitz.*)

RODRIGO. Hm, madam countess— (*Geschwitz starts and shrinks.*) Do I look as dangerous as that? (*To himself.*) I must make a bon mot. (*Aloud.*) May I perhaps make so bold—

GESCHWITZ. You can go to the devil!

CASTI-PIANI. (*As he leads Lulu in.*) Permit me a word or two.

LULU. (*Not noticing Rodrigo who presses his note into her hand.*) Oh, as many as you like. (*Rodrigo bows and goes out, rear.*)

CASTI-PIANI. (*To Geschwitz.*) Leave us alone!

LULU. (*To Casti-Piani.*) Have I hurt you again in any way?

CASTI-PIANI. (*Since Geschwitz does not stir.*) Are you deaf? (*Geschwitz, sighing deeply, goes out, rear.*)

LULU. Just say straight out how much you want.

CASTI-PIANI. With money you can no longer serve me.

LULU. What makes you think that we have no more money?

CASTI-PIANI. You handed out the last bit of it to me yesterday.

LULU. If you're sure of that then I suppose it's so.

CASTI-PIANI. You're down on the bare ground, you and your writer.

LULU. Then why all the words?—If you want to have me for yourself you need not first threaten me with execution.

CASTI-PIANI. I know that. But I've told you more than once that you won't be my downfall. I haven't sucked you dry because you loved me, but loved you in order to suck you. Bianetta is more to my taste from top to bottom than you. You set out the choicest sweetmeats, and after one has frittered his time away at them he finds he's hungrier than before. You've loved too long, even for our present relations. With a healthy young man, you only ruin his nervous system. But you'll fit all the more perfectly in the position I have sought out for you.

LULU. You're crazy! Have I commissioned you to find a position for me?

CASTI-PIANI. I told you, though, that I was an appointments-agent.

LULU. You told me you were a police spy.

CASTI-PIANI. One can't live on that alone. I was an appointments-agent originally, till I blundered over a minister's daughter I'd got a position for in Valparaiso. The little darling in her childhood's dreams imagined the life even more intoxicating than it is, and complained of it to Mama. On that, they nabbed me; but by reliable demeanor I soon enough won the confidence of the criminal police and they sent me here on a hundred and fifty marks a month, because they were tripling our contingent here on account of these everlasting bomb-explosions. But who can get along on a hundred and fifty marks a month? My colleagues get women to support them; but, of course, I found it more convenient to take up my former calling again; and of the numberless adventuresses of the best families of the entire world, whom chance brings together here, I have already forwarded many a young creature hungry for life to the place of her natural vocation.

LULU. (*Decisively.*) I wouldn't do in that business.

CASTI-PIANI. Your views on that question make no difference whatever to me. The department of justice will pay anyone who delivers the murderess of Dr. Schön into the hands of the police a thousand marks. I only need to whistle for the constable who's standing down at the corner to have earned a thousand marks. Against that, the House of Oikonomopulos in Cairo bids sixty pounds for you—twelve hundred marks—two hundred more than the Attorney General. And, besides, I am still so far a friend of mankind that I prefer to help my loves to happiness, not plunge them into misfortune.

LULU. (*As before.*) The life in such a house can never make a woman of my stamp happy. When I was fifteen, that might have happened to me. I was desperate then—thought I should never be happy. I bought a revolver, and ran one night bare-foot thru the deep snow over the bridge to the park to shoot myself there. But then by good luck I lay three months in the hospital without setting eyes on a man, and in that time my eyes opened and I got to know myself. Night after night in my dreams I saw the man for whom I was created and who was created for me, and then when I was let out on the men again I was no longer a silly goose. Since then I can see on a man, in a pitch-dark night and a hundred feet away, whether we're suited to each other; and if I sin against that insight I feel the next day dirtied, body and soul, and need weeks to get over the loathing I have for myself. And now you imagine I'll give myself to every and any Tom and Harry!

CASTI-PIANI. Toms and Harries don't patronize Oikonomopulos of Cairo. His custom consists of Scottish lords, Russian dignitaries, Indian governors, and our jolly Rhineland captains of industry. I must only guarantee that you speak French. With your gift for languages you'll quickly enough learn as much English, besides, as you'll need to get on with. And you'll reside in a royally furnished apartment with an outlook on the minarets of the El Azhar Mosque, and walk around all day on Persian carpets as thick as your fist, and dress every evening in a fabulous Paris gown and drink as much champagne as your customers can pay for, and, finally, you'll even remain, up to a certain point, your own mistress. If the man doesn't please you, you needn't bring him any reciprocal feelings. Just let him give in his card, and then— (*Shrugs, and snaps his fingers.*) If the ladies didn't get used to that the whole business would be simply impossible, because every one after the first four weeks would go headlong to the devil.

LULU. (*Her voice shaking.*) I do believe that since yesterday you've got a screw loose somewhere. Am I to understand that the Egyptian will pay fifteen hundred francs for a person whom he's never seen?

CASTI-PIANI. I took the liberty of sending him your pictures.

LULU. Those pictures that I gave you, you've sent to him?

CASTI-PIANI. You see he can value them better than I. The picture in which you stand before the mirror as Eve he'll probably hang up at the house-door, after you've got there. . . . And then there's one thing more for you to notice: with Oikonomopulos in Cairo you'll be safer from your blood-hounds than if you crept into a Canadian wilderness. It isn't so easy to transport an Egyptian courtesan to a German prison,—first, on account of the mere expense, and second, from fear of coming too close to eternal Justice.

LULU. (*Proudly, in a clear voice.*) What's your eternal Justice to do with me! You can see as plain as your five fingers I shan't let myself be locked up in any such amusement-place!

CASTI-PIANI. Then do you want me to whistle for the policeman?

LULU. (*In wonder.*) Why don't you simply ask me for twelve hundred marks, if you want the money?

CASTI-PIANI. I want for no money! And I also don't ask for it because you're dead broke.

LULU. We still have thirty thousand marks.

CASTI-PIANI. In Jungfrau-stock! I never have anything to do with stock. The Attorney-General pays in the national currency, and Oikonomopulos pays in English gold. You can be on board early to-morrow. The passage doesn't last much more than five days. In two weeks at most you're in safety. Here you are nearer to prison than anywhere. It's a wonder which I, as one of the secret police, cannot understand, that you two have been able to live for a full year unmolested. But just as I came on the track of your antecedents, so any day, with your mighty consumption of men, one of my colleagues may make the happy discovery. Then I may just wipe my mouth, and you spend in prison the most enjoyable years of your life. If you will kindly decide quickly. The train goes at 12.30. If we haven't struck a bargain before eleven, I whistle up the policeman. If we have, I pack you, just as you stand, into a carriage, drive you to the station, and to-morrow escort you on board ship.

LULU. But is it possible you can be serious in all this?

CASTI-PIANI. Don't you understand that I can act now only for your bodily rescue?

LULU. I'll go with you to America or to China, but I can't let myself be sold of my own accord! That is worse than prison!

CASTI-PIANI. (*Drawing a letter from his pocket.*) Just read this effusion! I'll read it to you. Here's the postmark "Cairo," so you won't believe I work with forged documents. The girl is a Berliner, was married two years and to a man whom you would have envied her, a former comrade of mine. He travels now for the Hamburg Colonial Company. . . .

LULU. (*Merrily.*) Then perhaps he visits his wife occasionally?

CASTI-PIANA. That is not incredible. But hear this impulsive expression of her feelings. My white-slave traffic seems to me absolutely no more honorable than the very best judge would tax it with being, but a cry of joy like this lets me feel a certain moral satisfaction for a moment. I am proud to earn my money by scattering happiness with full hands. (*Reads.*) "Dear Mr. Meyer"—that's my name as a white-slave trader—"when you go to Berlin, please go right away to the conservatory on the Potsdamer Strasse and ask for Gusti von Rosenkron—the most beautiful woman that I've ever seen in nature—delightful hands and feet, naturally small waist, straight back, full body, big eyes and short nose—just the sort you like best. I have written to her already. She has no prospects with her singing. Her mother hasn't a penny. Sorry she's already twenty-two, but she's pining for love. Can't marry, because absolutely without means. I have spoken with Madame. They'd like to take another German, if she's well educated and musical. Italians and Frenchwomen can't compete with us, 'cause of too little culture. If you should see Fritz"—Fritz is the husband; he's getting a divorce, of course,—"tell him it was all a bore. He didn't know any better, nor did I either." Now come the exact details—

LULU. (*Goaded.*) I can not sell the only thing that ever was my own!

CASTI-PIANI. Let me read some more.

LULU. (*As before.*) This very evening, I'll hand over to you our entire wealth.

CASTI-PIANI. Believe me, for God's sake, I've got your last red cent! If we haven't left this house before eleven, you and your lot will be transported to-morrow in a police-car to Germany.

LULU. You can't give me up!

CASTI-PIANI. Do you think that would be the worst thing I can have done in my life? . . . I must, in case we go to-night, have just a brief word with Bianetta. (*He goes into the card-room, leaving the door open behind him. Lulu stares before her, mechanically crumpling up the note that Rodrigo stuck into her hand, which she has held in her fingers thruout the dialog. Alva, behind the card-table, gets up, a bill in his hand, and comes into the salon.*)

ALVA. (*To Lulu.*) Brilliantly! It's going brilliantly! Geschwitz is wagering her last shirt. Puntschu has promised me ten more Jungfrau-shares. Steinherz is making her little gains and profits. (*Exit, lower right.*)

LULU. I in a bordell?—(*She reads the paper she holds, and laughs madly.*)

ALVA. (*Coming back with a cash-box in his hand.*) Aren't you going to play, too?

LULU. Oh, yes, surely—why not?

ALVA. By the way, it's in the Berliner Tageblatt to-day that Alfred Hugenberg has hurled himself over the stairs in prison.

LULU. Is he too in prison?

ALVA. Only in a sort of house of detention. (*Exit, rear. Lulu is about to follow, but Countess Geschwitz meets her in the door-way.*)

GESCHWITZ. You are going because I come?

LULU. (*Resolutely.*) No, God knows. But when you come then I go.

GESCHWITZ. You have defrauded me of all the good things of this world that I still possessed. You might at the very least preserve the outward forms of politeness in your intercourse with me.

LULU. (*As before.*) I am as polite to you as to any other woman. I only beg you to be equally so to me.

GESCHWITZ. Have you forgotten the passionate endearments by which, while we lay together in the hospital, you seduced me into letting myself be locked into prison for you?

LULU. Well, why else did you bring me down with the cholera beforehand? I swore very different things to myself, even while it was going on, from what I had to promise you! I am shaken with horror at the thought that that should ever become reality!

GESCHWITZ. Then you cheated me consciously, deliberately?

LULU. (*Gaily.*) What have you been cheated of, then? Your physical advantages have found so enthusiastic an admirer here, that I ask myself if I won't have to give piano lessons once more, to keep alive! No seventeen-year-old child could make a man madder with love than you, a pervert, are making him, poor fellow, by your shrewishness.

GESCHWITZ. Of whom are you speaking? I don't understand a word.

LULU. (*As before.*) I'm speaking of your acrobat, of Rodrigo Quast. He's an athlete: he balances two saddled cavalry horses on his chest. Can a woman desire anything more glorious? He told me just now that he'd jump into the water to-night if you did not take pity on him.

GESCHWITZ. I do not envy you this cleverness with which you torture the helpless victims sacrificed to you by their inscrutable destiny. My own plight has not yet wrung from me the pity that I feel for you. *I* feel free as a god when I think to what creatures *you* are enslaved.

LULU. Who do you mean?

GESCHWITZ. Casti-Piani, upon whose forehead the most degenerate baseness is written in letters of fire!

LULU. Be silent! I'll kick you, if you speak ill of *him*. He loves me with an uprightness against which your most venturous self-sacrifices are poor as beggary! He gives me such proofs of self-denial as reveal *you* for the first time in all your loathsomeness! You didn't get finished in your mother's womb, neither as woman nor as man. You have no human nature like the rest of us. The stuff didn't go far enough for a man, and for a woman you got too much brain into your skull. That's the reason you're crazy! Turn to Miss Bianetta! She can be had for everything for pay! Press a gold-piece into her hand and she'll belong to you. (*All the company save Kadidia throng in out of the card-room.*) For the Lord's sake, what has happened?

PUNTSCHU. Nothing whatever! We're thirsty, that's all.

MAGELONE. Everybody has won. We can't believe it.

BIANETTA. It seems I have won a whole fortune!

LUDMILLA. Don't boast of it, my child. That isn't lucky.

MAGELONE. But the bank has won, too! How is that possible?

ALVA. It is colossal, where all the money comes from!

CASTI-PIANI. Let us not ask! Enough that we need not spare the champagne.

HEILMANN. I can pay for a supper in a respectable restaurant afterwards, anyway!

ALVA. To the buffet, ladies! Come to the buffet! (*All exeunt, lower left.*)

RODRIGO. (*Holding Lulu back.*) Un momong, my heart. Have you read my billet-doux?

LULU. Threaten me with discovery as much as you like! I have no more twenty thousands to dispose of.

RODRIGO. Don't lie to me, you punk! You've still got forty thousand in Jungfrau-stock. Your so-called spouse has just been bragging of it himself!

LULU. Then turn to him with your blackmailing! It's all one to me what he does with his money.

RODRIGO. Thank you! With that blockhead I'd need twice twenty-four hours to make him grasp what I was talking about. And then come his explanations, that make one deathly sick; and meanwhile my bride writes me "It's all up!" and I can just hang a hurdy-gurdy over my shoulder.

LULU. Have you got engaged here, then?

RODRIGO. Maybe I ought to have asked your permission first? What were my thanks here that I freed you from prison at the cost of my health? You abandoned me! I might have had to be a baggage-man if this girl hadn't taken me up! At my very first entrance, right away, they threw a velvet-covered arm-chair at my head! This country is too decadent to value genuine shows of strength any more. If I'd been a boxing kangaroo they'd have interviewed me and put my picture in all the papers. Thank heaven, I'd already made the acquaintance of my Celestine. She's got the savings of twenty years deposited with the government; and she loves me just for myself. She doesn't aim only at vulgar things, like you. She's had three children by an American bishop—all of the greatest promise. Day after to-morrow we'll get married by the registrar.

LULU. You have my blessing.

RODRIGO. Your blessing can be stolen from me. I've told my bride I had twenty thousand in stock at the bank.

LULU. (*Amused.*) And after that he boasts the person loves him for himself!

RODRIGO. She honors in me the man of mind, not the man of might as you and all the others have done. That's over now. First they tore the clothes from one's body and then they waltzed around with the chambermaid. I'll be a skeleton before I'll let myself in again for such diversions!

LULU. Then why the devil do you pursue the unfortunate Geschwitz with your attentions?

RODRIGO. Because the creature is of noble blood. I'm a man of the world, and can do distinguished conversation better than any of you. But now (*with a gesture*) my talk is hanging out of my mouth! Will you get me the money before to-morrow evening or won't you?

LULU. I have no money.

RODRIGO. I'll have hen-droppings in my head before I'll let myself be put off with that! He'll give you his last cent if you'll only do your damned duty once! You lured the poor lad here, and now he can see where to scare up a suitable engagement for his accomplishments.

LULU. What has it to do with you if he wastes his money with women or at cards?

RODRIGO. Do you absolutely w a n t, then, to throw the last penny that his father earned by his paper into the jaws of this rapacious pack? You'll make four people happy if you'll not take things too exactly and sacrifice yourself for a beneficent purpose! Has it got to be only Casti-Piani f o r e v e r?

LULU. (*Lightly.*) Shall I ask him perhaps to light you down the stairs?

RODRIGO. As you wish, countess! If I don't get the twenty thousand marks by to-morrow evening, I make a statement to the police and your court has an end. Auf Wiedersehen! (*Heilmann enters, breathless, upper right.*)

LULU. You're looking for Miss Magelone? She's not here.

HEILMANN. No, I'm looking for something else—

RODRIGO. (*Taking him to the entry-door, opposite him.*) Second door on the left.

LULU. (*To Rodrigo.*) Did you learn that from your bride?

HEILMANN. (*Bumping into Puntschu in the doorway.*) Excuse me, my angel!

PUNTSCHU. Ah, it's you. Miss Magelone's waiting for you in the lift.

HEILMANN. You go up with her, please. I'll be right back. (*He hurries out, left. Lulu goes out at lower left. Rodrigo follows her.*)

PUNTSCHU. Some heat, that! If I don't cut off y o u r ears, you'll cut 'em off me! If I can't hire out my Jehoshaphat, I've just got to help myself with my brains! Won't they get wrinkled, my brains! Won't they get indisposed! Won't they need to bathe in Eau de Cologne! (*Bob, a groom in a red jacket, tight leather breeches, and twinkling riding-boots,* 15 *years old, brings in a telegram.*)

BOB. Mr. Puntschu, the banker!

PUNTSCHU. (*Breaks open the telegram and murmurs:*) "Jungfrau Funicular Stock fallen to—" Ay, ay, so goes the world! (*To Bob.*) Wait! (*Gives him a tip.*) Tell me—what's your name?

BOB. Well, it's really Freddy, but they call me Bob, because that's the fashion now.

PUNTSCHU. How old are you?

BOB. Fifteen.

KADIDIA. (*Enters hesitatingly from lower left.*) I beg your pardon, can you tell me if mama is here?

PUNTSCHU. No, my dear. (*Aside.*) Devil, she's got breeding!

KADIDIA. I'm hunting all over for her; I can't find her anywhere.

PUNTSCHU. Your mama will turn up again soon, as true as my name's Puntschu! (*Looking at Bob.*) And that pair of breeches! God of Justice! It gets uncanny! (*He goes out, upper right.*)

KADIDIA. Haven't y o u seen my mama, perhaps?

BOB. No, but you only need to come with me.

KADIDIA. Where is she then?

BOB. She's gone up in the lift. Come along.

KADIDIA. No, no, I can't go up with you.

BOB. We can hide up there in the corridor.

KADIDIA. No, no, I can't come, or I'll be scolded. (*Magelone, terribly excited, rushes in, upper left, and possesses herself of Kadidia.*)

MAGELONE. Ha, there you are at last, you common creature!

KADIDIA. (*Crying.*) O mama, mama, I was hunting for you!

MAGELONE. Hunting for me? Did I tell you to hunt for me? What have you had to do with this fellow? (*Heilmann, Alva, Ludmilla, Puntschu, Geschwitz, and Lulu enter, lower left. Bob has withdrawn.*) Now don't bawl before all the people on me; look out, I tell you!

LULU. (*As they all surround Kadidia.*) But you're crying, sweetheart! Why are you crying?

PUNTSCHU. By God, she's really been crying! Who's done anything to hurt you, little goddess?

LUDMILLA. (*Kneels before her and folds her in her arms.*) Tell me, cherub, what bad thing has happened. Do you want a cookie? Do you want some chocolate?

MAGELONE. It's just nerves. The child's getting them much too soon. It would be the best thing if no one paid any attention to her!

PUNTSCHU. That sounds like you! You're a pretty mother! The courts 'll yet take the child away from you and appoint me her guardian! (*Stroking Kadidia's cheeks.*) Isn't that so, my little goddess?

GESCHWITZ. I should be glad if we started the baccarat again at last? (*All go into the card-room. Lulu is held back at the door by Bob.*)

LULU. (*When Bob has whispered to her.*) Certainly! Let him come in! (*Bob opens the door and lets Schigolch enter, in evening dress, his patent-leather shoes much worn, and keeping on his shabby opera hat.*)

SCHIGOLCH. (*With a look at Bob.*) Where d'd you get him from?

LULU. The circus.

SCHIGOLCH. How much does he get?

LULU. Ask him if it interests you. (*To Bob.*) Shut the doors. (*Bob goes out lower left, shutting the door behind him.*)

SCHIGOLCH. (*Sitting down.*) The truth is, I'm in need of money. I've hired a flat for my mistress.

LULU. Have you taken another mistress here, too?

SCHIGOLCH. She's from Frankfort. In her youth she was mistress to the King of Naples. She tells me every day she was once very bewitching.

LULU. (*Outwardly with complete composure.*) Does she need the money very badly?

SCHIGOLCH. She wants to fit up her own apartments. Such sums are of no account to y o u. (*Lulu is suddenly overcome with a fit of weeping.*)

LULU. (*Flinging herself at Schigolch.*) O God Omnipotent!

SCHIGOLCH. (*Patting her.*) Well? What is it now?

LULU. (*Sobbing violently.*) It's too horrible!

SCHIGOLCH. (*Draws her onto his knee and holds her in his arms like a little child.*) Hm—You're trying to do too much, child. You must go to bed, now and then, with a story.—Cry, that's right, cry it all out. It used to shake you just so fifteen years ago. Nobody has screamed since then, the way you could scream! You didn't wear any white tufts on your head then, nor any transparent stockings on your legs: you had neither shoes nor stockings then.

LULU. (*Crying.*) Take me home with you! Take me home with you to-night! Please! We'll find carriages enough downstairs!

SCHIGOLCH. I'll take you with me; I'll take you with me.—What is it?

LULU. It's going round my neck! I'm to be shown up!

SCHIGOLCH. By who? Who's showing you up?

LULU. The acrobat.

SCHIGOLCH. (*With the utmost composure.*) I'll look after him.

LULU. Look after him! P l e a s e, look after him! Then do with me what you will!

SCHIGOLCH. If he comes to me, he's done for. My window is over the water. But (*shaking his head*) he won't come; he won't come.

LULU. What number do you live at?

SCHIGOLCH. 376, the last house before the hippodrome.

LULU. I'll send him there. He'll come with the crazy person that creeps about my feet. He'll come this very evening. Go home and let them find it comfortable.

SCHIGOLCH. Just let them come.

LULU. To-morrow bring the gold rings he wears in his ears.

SCHIGOLCH. Has he got rings in his ears?

LULU. You can take them out before you let him down. He doesn't notice anything when he's drunk.

SCHIGOLCH. And then, child—what then?

LULU. Then I'll give you the money for your mistress.

SCHIGOLCH. I call that pretty stingy.

LULU. And whatever else you want! What I have!

SCHIGOLCH. It's pretty near ten years since we knew each other.

LULU. Is that all?—But you've got a mistress.

SCHIGOLCH. My Frankforter is no longer of to-day.

LULU. But then swear!

SCHIGOLCH. Haven't I always kept my word to you?

LULU. Swear that you'll look after him!

SCHIGOLCH. I'll look after him.

LULU. Swear it to me! Swear it to me!

SCHIGOLCH. (*Puts his hand on her ankle.*) By everything that's holy! To-night, if he comes—

LULU. By everything that's holy!—How cool that is!

SCHIGOLCH. How hot this is!

LULU. Drive straight home. They'll come in half-an-hour! Take a carriage!

SCHIGOLCH. I'm going.

LULU. Quick! Please!— —All-powerful—

SCHIGOLCH. Why do you stare at me so again already?

LULU. Nothing— . . .

SCHIGOLCH. Well? Is your tongue frozen on you?

LULU. My garter's broken.

SCHIGOLCH. What if it is? Is that all?

LULU. What does that augur?

SCHIGOLCH. What does it? I'll fasten it for you if you'll keep still.

LULU. That augurs misfortune!

SCHIGOLCH. (*Yawning.*) Not for you, child. Cheer up, I'll look after him! (*Exit. Lulu puts her left foot on a foot-stool, fastens her garter, and goes out into the card-room. Then Rodrigo is cuffed in from the dining-room, lower left, by Casti-Piani.*)

RODRIGO. You can treat me decently anyway!

CASTI-PIANI. (*Still perfectly unemotional.*) Whatever would induce me to do that? I will know what you said to her here a little while ago.

RODRIGO. Then you can be very fond of me!

CASTI-PIANI. Will you bandy words with me, dog? You demanded that she go up in the lift with you!

RODRIGO. That's a shameless, perfidious lie!

CASTI-PIANI. She told me so herself. You threatened to denounce her if she didn't go with you.—Shall I shoot you on the spot?

RODRIGO. The shameless hussy! As if anything like that could occur to me!—Even if I should want to have her, God knows I don't first need to threaten her with prison!

CASTI-PIANI. Thank you. That's all I wanted to know. (*Exit, upper left.*)

RODRIGO. Such a hound! A fellow I could throw up onto the roof so he'd stick like a Limburger cheese!—Come back here, so I can wind your guts round your neck. That would be even better!

LULU. (*Enters, lower left; merrily.*) Where were you? I've been hunting for you like a pin.

RODRIGO. I've shown him what it means to start anything with me!

LULU. Whom?

RODRIGO. Your Casti-Piani! What made you tell him, you slut, that I wanted to seduce you?!

LULU. Did you not ask me to give myself to my deceased husband's son for twenty thousand in Jungfrau shares?

RODRIGO. Because it's your duty to take pity on the poor young fellow! You shot away his father before his nose in the very best years of life! But your Casti-Piani will think it over before he comes into my sight again.

I gave him one in the basket that made the tripes fly to heaven like Roman candles. If you've got no better substitute for me, then I'm sorry ever to have had your favor!

LULU. Lady Geschwitz is in the fearfullest case. She twists herself up in fits. She's at the point of jumping into the water if you let her wait any longer.

RODRIGO. What's the beast waiting for?

LULU. For you, to take her with you.

RODRIGO. Then give her my regards, and she can jump into the water.

LULU. She'll lend me twenty thousand marks to save me from destruction if you will preserve her from it herself. If you'll take her off to-night, I'll deposit twenty thousand marks to-morrow in your name at any bank you say.

RODRIGO. And if I don't take her off with me?

LULU. Denounce me! Alva and I are dead broke.

RODRIGO. Devil and damnation!

LULU. You make four people happy if you don't take things too exactly and sacrifice yourself for a beneficent purpose.

RODRIGO. That won't go; I know that, beforehand. I've tried that out enough now. Who counts on an honorable soul like that in a bag o' bones! What the person had for me was her being an aristocrat. My behavior was as gentleman-like, and more, as you could find among German circus-people. If I'd only just pinched her in the calves once!

LULU. (*Watchfully.*) She is still a virgin.

RODRIGO. (*Sighing.*) If there's a God in heaven, you'll get paid for your jokes some day! I prophesy that.

LULU. Geschwitz waits. What shall I tell her?

RODRIGO. My very best wishes, and I am perverse.

LULU. I will deliver that.

RODRIGO. Wait a sec. Is it certain sure I get twenty thousand marks from her?

LULU. Ask herself!

RODRIGO. Then tell her I'm ready. I await her in the dining-room. I must just first look after a barrel of caviare. (*Exit, left. Lulu opens the rear door and calls in a clear voice "Martha!" Countess Geschwitz enters, closing the door behind her.*)

LULU. (*Pleased.*) Dear heart, you can save me from death to-night.

GESCHWITZ. How?

LULU. By going to a certain house with the acrobat.

GESCHWITZ. What for, dear?

LULU. He says you must belong to him this very night or he'll denounce me to-morrow.

GESCHWITZ. You know I can't belong to any man. My fate has not permitted that.

LULU. If you don't please him, that's his own fix. Why has he fallen in love with you?

GESCHWITZ. But he'll get as brutal as a hangman. He'll revenge himself for his disappointment and beat my head in. I've been thru that already. . . . Can you not possibly spare me this hardest test?

LULU. What will you gain by his denouncing me?

GESCHWITZ. I have still enough of my fortune to take us to America together in the steerage. There you'd be safe from all your pursuers.

LULU. (*Pleased and gay.*) I want to stay here. I can never be happy in any other city. You must tell him that you can't live without him. Then he'll feel flattered and be gentle as a lamb. You must pay the coachman, too: give him this paper with the address on it. 376 is a sixth-class hotel where they're expecting you with him this evening.

GESCHWITZ. (*Shuddering.*) How can such a monstrosity save your life? I don't understand that. You have conjured up to torture me the most terrible fate that can fall upon outlawed me!

LULU. (*Watchful.*) Perhaps the encounter will cure you.

GESCHWITZ. (*Sighing.*) O Lulu, if an eternal retribution does exist, I hope I may not have to answer then for you. I cannot make myself believe that no God watches over us. Yet you are probably right that there is nothing there, for how can an insignificant worm like me have provoked his wrath so as to experience only horror there where all living creation swoons for bliss?

LULU. You needn't complain. When you a r e happy you're a hundred thousand times happier than one of us ordinary mortals ever is!

GESCHWITZ. I know that too! I envy no one! But I am still waiting. You have deceived me so often already.

LULU. I am yours, my darling, if you quiet Mr. Acrobat till to-morrow. He only wants his vanity placated. You must beseech him to take pity on you.

GESCHWITZ. And to-morrow?

LULU. I await you, my heart. I shall not open my eyes till you come: see no chambermaid, receive no hairdresser, not open my eyes before you are with me.

GESCHWITZ. Then let him come.

LULU. But you must throw yourself at his head, dear! Have you got the house-number?

GESCHWITZ. Three-seventy-six. But quick now!

LULU. (*Calls into the dining-room.*) Ready, my darling?

RODRIGO. (*Entering.*) The ladies will pardon my mouth's being full.

GESCHWITZ. (*Seizing his hand.*) I implore you, have mercy on my need!

RODRIGO. A la bonne heure! Let us mount the scaffold! (*Offers her his arm.*)

LULU. Good-night, children! (*Accompanies them into the corridor. . . . then quickly returns with Bob.*) Quick, quick, Bob! We must get away this moment! You escort me! But we must change clothes!

BOB. (*Curt and clear.*) As the gracious lady bids.

LULU. Oh what, gracious lady! You give me your clothes and put on mine. Come! (*Exeunt into the dining-room. Noise in the card-room, the doors are torn open, and Puntschu, Heilmann, Alva, Bianetta, Magelone, Kadidia and Ludmilla enter, Heilmann holding a piece of paper with a glowing Alpine peak at its top.*)

HEILMANN. (*To Puntschu.*) Will you accept this share of Jungfrau-stock, sir?

PUNTSCHU. But that paper has no exchange, my friend.

HEILMANN. You rascal! You just don't want to give me my revenge!

MAGELONE. (*To Bianetta.*) Have you any idea what it's all about?

LUDMILLA. Puntschu has taken all his money from him, and now gives up the game.

HEILMANN. Now he's got cold feet, the filthy Jew!

PUNTSCHU. How have I given up the game? How have I got cold feet? The gentleman has merely to lay plain cash! Is this my banking-office I'm in? He can proffer me his trash to-morrow morning!

HEILMANN. Trash you call that? The stock in my knowledge is at 210!

PUNTSCHU. Yesterday it was at 210, you're right. To-day, it's just nowhere. And to-morrow you'll find nothing cheaper or more tasteful to paper your stairs with.

ALVA. But how is that possible? Then we would be down and out!

PUNTSCHU. Well, what am *I* to say, who have lost my whole fortune in it! To-morrow morning I shall have the pleasure of taking up the struggle for an assured existence for the thirty-sixth time!

MAGELONE. (*Passing forward.*) Am I dreaming or do I really hear the Jungfrau-stock has fallen?

PUNTSCHU. Fallen even lower than you! Tho you can use 'em for curl-paper.

MAGELONE. O God in Heaven! Ten years' work! (*Falls in a faint.*)

KADIDIA. Wake up, mama! Wake up!

BIANETTA. Say, Mr. Puntschu, where will you eat this evening, since you've lost your whole fortune?

PUNTSCHU. Wherever you like, young lady! Take me where you will, but quickly! Here it's getting frightful. (*Exeunt Puntschu and Bianetta.*)

HEILMANN. (*Squeezing up his stock and flinging it to the ground.*) That is what one gets from this pack!

LUDMILLA. Why do you speculate on the Jungfrau too? Send a few little notices on the company to the German police here, and then you'll still win something in the end.

HEILMANN. I've never tried that in my life, but if you want to help me—?

LUDMILLA. Let's go to an all-night restaurant. Do you know the Five-footed Calf?

HEILMAN. I'm very sorry—

LUDMILLA. Or the Sucking Lamb, or the Smoking Dog? They're all right near here. We'll be all by ourselves there, and before dawn we'll have a little article ready.

HEILMANN. Don't you sleep?

LUDMILLA. Oh, of course; but not at night. (*Exeunt Heilmann and Ludmilla.*)

ALVA. (*Who has been trying to resuscitate Magelone.*) Ice-cold hands! Ah, what a splendid woman! We must undo her waist. Come, Kadidia, undo your mother's waist! She's so fearfully tight-laced.

KADIDIA. (*Without stirring.*) I'm afraid. (*Lulu enters lower left in a jockey-cap, red jacket, white leather breeches and riding boots, a riding cape over her shoulders.*)

LULU. Have you any cash, Alva?

ALVA. (*Looking up.*) Have you gone crazy?

LULU. In two minutes the police'll be here. We are denounced. You can stay of course, if you're eager to!

ALVA. (*Springing up.*) Merciful Heaven! (*Exeunt Alva and Lulu.*)

KADIDIA. (*Shaking her mother, in tears.*) Mama, Mama! Wake up! They've all run away!

MAGELONE. (*Coming to herself.*) And youth gone! And my best days gone! Oh, this life!

KADIDIA. But I'm young, mama! Why shouldn't I earn any money? I don't want to go back to the convent! Please, mama, keep me with you!

MAGELONE. God bless you, sweetheart! You don't know what you say— Oh, no, I shall look around for an engagement in a Varieté, and sing the people my misfortunes with the Jungfrau-stock. Things like that are always applauded.

KADIDIA. But you've got no voice, mama!

MAGELONE. Ah, yes, that's true!

KADIDIA. Take me with you to the Varieté!

MAGELONE. No, it would break my heart!—But, well, if it can't be otherwise, and you're so made for it,—I can't change things!—Yes, we can go to the Olympia together to-morrow!

KADIDIA. O mama, how glad that makes me feel! (*A plain-clothes detective enters, upper left.*)

DETECTIVE. In the name of the law—I arrest you!

CASTI-PIANI. (*Following him, bored.*) What sort of nonsense is that? T h a t isn't the right one!

CURTAIN.

ACT III

An attic room, without windows, but with two skylights, under one of which stands a bowl filled with rain-water. Down right, a door thru a board partition into a sort of cubicle under the slanting roof. Near it, a wobbly flower-table with a bottle and a smoking oil-lamp on it. Upper right, a worn-out couch. Door centre; near it, a chair without a seat. Down left, below the entrance door, a torn gray mattress. None of the doors can shut tight.

The rain beats on the roof. Schigolch in a long gray overcoat lies on the mattress; Alva on the couch, wrapped in a plaid whose straps still hang on the wall above him.

SCHIGOLCH. The rain's drumming for the parade.

ALVA. Cheerful weather for her first appearance! I dreamt just now we were dining together at Olympia. Bianetta was still with us. The table-cloth was dripping on all four sides with champagne.

SCHIGOLCH. Ya, ya. And I was dreaming of a Christmas pudding. (*Lulu appears, back, barefoot, in a torn black dress, but with her hair falling to her shoulders.*) Where have you been? Curling your hair first?

ALVA. She only does that to revive old memories.

LULU. If one could only get warmed, just a little, from one of you!

ALVA. Will you enter barefoot on your pilgrimage?

SCHIGOLCH. The first step always costs all kinds of moaning and groaning. Twenty years ago it was no whit better, and what she has learned since then! The coals only have to be blown. When she's been at it a week, not ten locomotives will hold her in our miserable attic.

ALVA. The bowl is running over.

LULU. What shall I do with the water?

ALVA. Pour it out the window. (*Lulu gets up on the chair and empties the bowl thru the sky-light.*)

LULU. It looks as if the rain would let up at last.

SCHIGOLCH. Your wasting the time when the clerks go home after supper.

LULU. Would to God I were lying somewhere where no step would wake me any more!

ALVA. Would I were, too! Why prolong this life? Let's rather starve to death together this very evening in peace and concord! Is it not the last stage now?

LULU. Why don't y o u go out and get us something to eat? You've never earned a penny in your whole life!

ALVA. In this weather, when no one would kick a dog from his door?

LULU. But me! I, with the little blood I have left in my limbs, I am to stop your mouths!

ALVA. I don't touch a farthing of the money!

SCHIGOLCH. Let her go, just! I long for one more Christmas pudding; then I've had enough.

ALVA. And I long for one more beefsteak and a cigarette; then die! I was just dreaming of a cigarette, such as has never yet been smoked!

SCHIGOLCH. She'll see us put an end to before her eyes, before doing herself a little pleasure.

LULU. The people on the street will sooner leave cloak and coat in my hands than go with me for nothing! If you hadn't sold my clothes, I at least wouldn't need to be afraid of the lamp-light. I'd like to see the woman who could earn anything in the rags I'm wearing on my body!

ALVA. I have left nothing human untried. As long as I had money I spent whole nights making up tables with which one couldn't help winning against the cleverest card-sharps. And yet evening after evening I lost more than if I had shaken out gold by the pailful. Then I offered my services to the courtesans; but they don't take anyone without the stamps of the courts, and they see at the first glance if one's related to the guillotine or not.

SCHIGOLCH. Ya, ya.

ALVA. I spared myself no disillusionments; but when I made jokes, they laughed at m e, and when I behaved as respectable as I am, they boxed my ears, and when I tried being smutty, they got so chaste and maidenly that my hair stood up on my head for horror. He who has not prevailed over society, they have no confidence in.

SCHIGOLCH. Won't you kindly put on your boots now, child? I don't think I shall grow much older in this lodging. It's months since I had any feeling in the ends of my toes. Toward midnight, I'll drink a bit more down in the pub. The lady that keeps it told me yesterday I seemed to really want to be her lover.

LULU. In the name of the three devils, I'll go down! (*She puts to her mouth the bottle on the flower-table.*)

SCHIGOLCH. So they can smell your stink a half-hour off!

LULU. I shan't drink it all.

ALVA. You won't go down. You're my woman. You shan't go down. I forbid it!

LULU. What would you forbid your woman when you can't support yourself?

ALVA. Whose fault is that? Who but my woman has laid me on the sick-bed?

LULU. Am I sick?

ALVA. Who has trailed me thru the dung? Who has made me my father's murderer?

LULU. Did *you* shoot him? He didn't lose much, but when I see you lying there I could hack off both my hands for having sinned so against my judgment! (*She goes out, into her room.*)

ALVA. She infected me from her Casti-Piani. It's a long time since she was susceptible to it herself!

SCHIGOLCH. Little devils like her can't begin putting up with it too soon, if angels are ever going to come out of them.

ALVA. She ought to have been born Empress of Russia. Then she'd have been in the right place. A second Catherine the Second! (*Lulu re-enters with a worn-out pair of boots, and sits on the floor to put them on.*)

LULU. If only I don't go headfirst down the stairs! Ugh, how cold! Is there anything in the world more dismal than a daughter of joy?

SCHIGOLCH. Patience, patience! She's only got to take the right road into the business at the start.

LULU. It's all right with me! Nothing's wrong with me any more. (*Puts the bottle to her lips.*) That warms one! O accursed! (*Exit.*)

SCHIGOLCH. When we hear her coming, we must creep into my cubby-hole awhile.

ALVA. I'm damned sorry for her! When I think back. . . . I grew up with her in a way, you know.

SCHIGOLCH. She'll hold out as long as I live, anyway.

ALVA. We treated each other at first like brother and sister. Mama was still living then. I met her by chance one morning when she was dressing. Dr. Goll had been called for a consultation. Her hair-dresser had read my first poem, that I'd had printed in "Society": "Follow thy pack far over the mountains; it will return again, covered with sweat and dust—"

SCHIGOLCH. Oh, ya!

ALVA. And then she came, in rose-colored muslin, with nothing under it but a white satin slip—for the Spanish ambassador's ball. Dr. Goll seemed to feel his death near. He asked me to dance with her, so she shouldn't cause any mad acts. Papa meanwhile never turned his eyes from us, and all thru the waltz she was looking over my shoulder, only at him. . . . Afterwards she shot him. It is unbelievable.

SCHIGOLCH. I've only got a very strong doubt whether anyone will bite any more.

ALVA. I shouldn't like to advise it to anybody! (*Schigolch grunts.*) At that time, tho she was a fully developed woman, she had the expression of a five-year-old, joyous, utterly healthy child. And she was only three years younger than me then—but how long ago it is now! For all her immense superiority in matters of practical life, she let me explain "Tristan and Isolde" to her—and how entrancingly she could listen! Out of the little sister who at her marriage still felt like a school-girl, came the unhappy, hysterical artist's wife. Out of the artist's wife came then the spouse of my blessed father, and out of h e r came, then, my mistress. Well, so that is the way of the world. Who will prevail against it?

SCHIGOLCH. If only she doesn't skid away from the gentlemen with honorable intentions and bring us up instead some vagabond she's exchanged her heart's secrets with.

ALVA. I kissed her for the first time in her rustling

bridal dress. But afterwards she didn't remember it. . . . All the same, I believe she had thought of me even in my father's arms. It can't have been often with him: he had his best time behind him, and she deceived him with coachman and boot-black; but when she did give herself to him, then *I* stood before her soul. Thru that, too, without my realizing it, she attained this dreadful power over me.

SCHIGOLCH. There they are! (*Heavy steps are heard mounting the stairs.*)

ALVA. (*Starting up.*) I will not endure it! I'll throw the fellow out!

SCHIGOLCH. (*Wearily picks himself up, takes Alva by the collar and cuffs him toward the left.*) Forward, forward! How is the young man to confess his trouble to her with us two sprawling round here?

ALVA. But if he demands other things—low things—of her?

SCHIGOLCH. If, well, if! What more will he demand of her? He's only a man like the rest of us!

ALVA. We must leave the door open.

SCHIGOLCH. (*Pushing Alva in, right.*) Nonsense! Lie down!

ALVA. I'll hear it soon enough. Heaven spare him!

SCHIGOLCH. (*Closing the door, from inside.*) Shut up!

ALVA. (*Faintly.*) He'd better look out! (*Lulu enters, followed by Hunidei, a gigantic figure with a smooth-shaven, rosy face, sky-blue eyes, and a friendly smile. He wears a tall hat and overcoat and carries a dripping umbrella.*)

LULU. Here's where I live. (*Hunidei puts his finger to his lips and looks at Lulu significantly. Then he opens his umbrella and puts it on the floor, rear, to dry.*) Of course, I know it isn't very comfortable here. (*Hunidei comes forward and puts his hand over her mouth.*) What do you mean me to understand by that? (*Hunidei puts his hand over her mouth, and his finger to his lips.*) I don't know what that means. (*Hunidei quickly stops her mouth. Lulu frees herself.*) We're quite alone here. No one will hear us. (*Hunidei lays his finger on his lips, shakes his head, points at Lulu, opens his mouth as if to speak, points at himself and then at the door.*) Herr Gott, he's a monster! (*Hunidei stops her mouth; then goes rear, folds up his overcoat and lays it over the chair near the door; then comes down with a broad smile, takes Lulu's head in both his hands and kisses her on the forehead. The door, right, half opens.*)

SCHIGOLCH. (*Behind the door.*) He's got a screw loose.

ALVA. He'd better look out!

SCHIGOLCH. She couldn't have brought up anything drearier!

LULU. (*Stepping back.*) I hope you're going to give me something! (*Hunidei stops her mouth and presses a gold-piece in her hand, then looks at her uncertain, questioningly, as she examines it and throws it from one hand to the other.*)

LULU. All right, it's good. (*Puts it into her pocket. Hunidei quickly stops her mouth, gives her a few silver coins, and glances at her commandingly.*) Oh, that's nice of you! (*Hunidei leaps madly about the room, brandishing his arms and staring upward in despair. Lulu cautiously nears him, throws an arm round him and kisses him on the mouth. Laughing soundlessly, he frees himself from her and looks questioningly. She takes up the lamp and opens the door to her room. He goes in smiling, tak-*

ing off his hat. The stage is dark save for what light comes thru the cracks of the door. Alva and Schigolch creep out on all fours.)

ALVA. They're gone.

SCHIGOLCH. (*Behind him.*) Wait.

ALVA. One can hear nothing here.

SCHIGOLCH. You've heard that often enough!

ALVA. I will kneel before her door.

SCHIGOLCH. Little mother's sonny! (*Presses past Alva, gropes across the stage to Hunidei's coat, and searches the pockets. Alva crawls to Lulu's door.*) Gloves, nothing more! (*Turns the coat round, searches the inside pockets, pulls a book out that he gives to Alva.*) Just see what that is. (*Alva holds the book to the light.*)

ALVA. (*Wearily deciphering the title-page.*) Warnings to pious pilgrims and such as wish to be so. Very helpful. Price, 2 s. 6 d.

SCHIGOLCH. It looks to me as if God had left him pretty completely. (*Lays the coat over the chair again and makes for the cubby-hole.*) There's nothing doing with these people. The country's best time's behind it!

ALVA. Life is never as bad as it's painted. (*He, too, creeps back.*)

SCHIGOLCH. Not even a silk muffler he's got and yet in Germany we creep on our bellies before this rabble.

ALVA. Come, let's vanish again.

SCHIGOLCH. She only thinks of herself, and takes the first man that runs across her path. Hope the dog remembers her the rest of his life! (*They disappear, left, shutting the door behind them. Lulu re-enters, setting the lamp on the table. Hunidei follows.*)

LULU. Will you come to see me again? (*Hunidei stops her mouth. She looks upward in a sort of despair and shakes her head. Hunidei, putting his coat on, approaches her grinning; she throws her arms around his neck; he gently frees himself, kisses her hand, and turns to the door. She starts to accompany him, but he signs to her to stay behind and noiselessly leaves the room. Schigolch and Alva re-enter.*)

LULU. (*Tonelessly.*) How he has stirred me up!

ALVA. How much did he give you?

LULU. (*As before.*) Here it is! All! Take it! I'm going down again.

SCHIGOLCH. We can still live like princes up here.

ALVA. He's coming back.

SCHIGOLCH. Then let's just retire again, quick.

ALVA. He's after his prayer-book. Here it is. It must have fallen out of his coat.

LULU. (*Listening.*) No, that isn't he. That's some one else.

ALVA. Some one's coming up. I hear it quite plainly.

LULU. Now there's some one tapping at the door. Who may that be?

SCHIGOLCH. Probably a good friend he's recommended us to. Come in! (*Countess Geschwitz enters, in poor clothes, with a canvas roll in her hand.*)

GESCHWITZ. (*To Lulu.*) If I've come at a bad time, I'll turn around again. The truth is, I haven't spoken to a living soul for ten days. I must just tell you right off, I haven't got any money. My brother never answered me at all.

SCHIGOLCH. Your ladyship would now like to stretch her feet out under our table?

LULU. (*Tonelessly.*) I'm going down again.

GESCHWITZ. Where are you going in this pomp?—However, I come not wholly empty-handed. I bring you something else. On my way here an old-clothes man offered me twelve shillings for it, but I could not force myself to part from it. You can sell it, though, if you want to.

SCHIGOLCH. What is it?

ALVA. Let us see it. (*Takes the canvas and unrolls it. Visibly rejoiced.*) Oh, by God, it's Lulu's portrait!

LULU. (*Screaming.*) Monster, you brought that here? Get it out of my sight! Throw it out of the window!

ALVA. (*Suddenly with renewed life, deeply pleased.*) Why, I should like to know? Looking on this picture I regain my self-respect. It makes my fate comprehensible to me. Everything we have endured gets clear as day. (*In a somewhat elegiac strain.*) Let him who feels secure in his middle-class position when he sees these blossoming pouting lips, these child-eyes, big and innocent, this rose-white body abounding in life,—let him cast the first stone at us!

SCHIGOLCH. We must nail it up. It will make an excellent impression on our patrons.

ALVA. (*Energetic.*) There's a nail sticking all ready for it in the wall.

SCHIGOLCH. But how did you come upon this acquisition?

GESCHWITZ. I secretly cut it out of the wall in your house, there, after you were gone.

ALVA. Too bad the color's got rubbed off round the edges. You didn't roll it up carefully enough. (*Fastens it to a high nail in the wall.*)

SCHIGOLCH. It's got to have another one underneath if it's going to hold. It makes the whole flat look more elegant.

ALVA. Let me alone; I know how I'll do it. (*He tears several nails out of the wall, pulls off his left boot, and with its heel nails the edges of the picture to the wall.*)

SCHIGOLCH. It's just got to hang a while again, to get its proper effect. Whoever looks at that'll imagine afterwards he's been in an Indian harem.

ALVA. (*Putting on his boot again, standing up proudly.*) Her body was at its highest point of development when that picture was painted. The lamp, kid dear! Seems to me it's got extraordinarily dark.

GESCHWITZ. He must have been an eminently gifted artist who painted that!

LULU. (*Perfectly composed again, stepping before the picture with the lamp.*) Didn't you know him, then?

GESCHWITZ. No. It must have been long before my time. I only occasionally heard chance remarks of yours, that he had cut his throat from persecution-mania.

ALVA. (*Comparing the picture with Lulu.*) The child-like expression in the eyes is still absolutely the same in spite of all she has lived thru since. (*In joyous excitement.*) The dewy freshness that covered her skin, the sweet-smelling breath from her lips, the rays of light that beam from her white forehead, and this challenging splendor of young flesh in throat and arms—

SCHIGOLCH. All that's gone with the rubbish wagon. She can say with self-assurance: That was me once! The man she falls into the hands of to-day 'll have no conception of what we were when we were young.

ALVA. (*Cheerfully.*) God be thanked, we don't notice the continual decline when we see a person all the time. (*Lightly.*) The woman blooms for us in the moment when she hurls the man to destruction for the rest of his life. That is her nature and her destiny.

SCHIGOLCH. Down in the street-lamp's shimmer she's still a match for a dozen walking spectres. The man who still wants to make connections at this hour looks out more for heart-qualities than mere physical good points. He decides for the pair of eyes from which the least thievery sparkles.

LULU. (*Now as pleased as Alva.*) I shall see if you're right. Adieu.

ALVA. (*In sudden anger.*) You shall not go down again, as I live!

GESCHWITZ. Where do you want to go?

ALVA. Down to fetch up a man.

GESCHWITZ. Lulu!

ALVA. She's done it once to-day already.

GESCHWITZ. Lulu, Lulu, where you go I go too.

SCHIGOLCH. If you want to put your bones up for sale, kindly get a district of your own!

GESCHWITZ. Lulu, I shall not stir from your side! I have weapons upon me.

SCHIGOLCH. Confound it all, her ladyship plots to fish with our bait!

LULU. You're killing me. I can't stand it here any more. (*Exit.*)

GESCHWITZ. You need fear nothing. I am with you. (*Follows her.*)

ALVA. (*Whimpering, throws himself on his couch. Schigolch swears, loudly and grumbling.*) I guess there's not much more good to expect on this side!

SCHIGOLCH. We ought to have held the creature back by the throat. She'll scare away everything that breathes with her aristocratic death's head.

ALVA. She's flung me onto a sick-bed and larded me with thorns outside and in!

SCHIGOLCH. And she's still got enough strength in her body to do the same for ten men alright.

ALVA. No mortally wounded man'll ever find the stab of mercy welcomer than I!

SCHIGOLCH. If she hadn't enticed the acrobat to my place that time, we'd have him round our necks to-day too.

ALVA. I see it swinging above my head as Tantalus saw the branch with the golden apples!

SCHIGLOCH. (*On his mattress.*) Won't you turn up the lamp a little?

ALVA. Can a simple, natural man in the wilderness suffer so unspeakably?!—God, God, what have I made of my life!

SCHIGOLCH. What's the beastly weather made of my ulster! When I was five-and-twenty, I knew how to help myself!

ALVA. It has not cost everyone my sunny, glorious youth!

SCHIGOLCH. I guess it'll go out in a minute. Till they come back it'll be as dark in here again as in mother's womb.

ALVA. With the clearest consciousness of my purpose I sought intercourse with people who'd never read a book in their lives. With self-denial, with exaltation, I clung to the elements, that I might be carried to the loftiest heights of poetic fame. The reckoning was false. I am the martyr of my calling. Since the death of my father I have not written a single line!

SCHIGOLCH. If only they haven't stayed together! Nobody but a silly boy will go with two, no matter what.

ALVA. They've not stayed together!

SCHIGOLCH. That's what I hope. If need be, she'll keep the creature off from her with kicks.

ALVA. One, risen from the dregs, is the most celebrated man of his nation; another, born in the purple, lies in the mud and cannot die!

SCHIGOLCH. Here they come!

ALVA. And what blessed hours of mutual joy in creation they had lived thru with each other!

SCHIGOLCH. They can do that now, for the first time rightly.—We must hide again.

ALVA. I stay here.

SCHIGOLCH. Just what do you pity them for?—Who spends his money has his good reasons for it!

ALVA. I have no longer the moral courage to let my comfort be disturbed for a miserable sum of money! (*He wraps himself up in his plaid.*)

SCHIGOLCH. Noblesse oblige! A respectable man does what he owes his position. (*He hides, left. Lulu opens the door, saying "Come right in, dearie," and there enters Prince Kungu Poti, heir-apparent of Uahubee, in a light suit, white spats, tan button-boots, and a gray tall hat. His speech, interrupted with frequent hiccoughs, abounds with the peculiar African hiss-sounds.*)

KUNGU POTI. God damn—it's dark on the stairs!

LULU. It's lighter here, sweetheart. (*Pulling him forward by the hand.*) Come on!

KUNGU POTI. But it's cold here, awful cold!

LULU. Have some brandy?

KUNGU POTI. Brandy? You bet—always! Brandy's good!

LULU. (*Giving him the bottle.*) I don't know where there's a glass.

KUNGU POTI. Doesn't matter. (*Drinks.*) Brandy! Lots of it!

LULU. You're a nice-looking young man.

KUNGU POTI. My father's the emperor of Uahubee. I've got six wives here, two Spanish, two English, two French. Well—I don't like my wives. Always I must take a bath, take a bath, take a bath. . . .

LULU. How much will you give me?

KUNGU POTI. Gold! Trust me, you shall have gold! One gold-piece. I always give gold-pieces.

LULU. You can give it to me later, but show it to me.

KUNGU POTI. I never pay beforehand.

LULU. But you can show it to me, thoh!

KUNGU POTI. Don't understand, don't understand! Come, Ragapsishimulara! (*Seizing Lulu round the waist.*) Come on!

LULU. (*Defending herself with all her strength.*) Let me be! Let me be! (*Alva, who has risen painfully from his couch, sneaks up to Kungu Poti from behind and pulls him back by the collar.*)

KUNGU POTI. (*Whirling round.*) Oh! Oh! This is a murder-hole! Come, my friend, I'll put you to sleep! (*Strikes him over the head with a loaded cane. Alva groans and falls in a heap.*) Here's a sleeping-draught! Here's opium for you! Sweet dreams to you! Sweet dreams! (*Then he gives Lulu a kiss; pointing to Alva.*) He dreams of you, Ragapsishimulara! Sweet dreams! (*Rushing to the door.*) Here's the door!! (*Exit.*)

LULU. But I'll not stay here?!—Who can stand it here now!—Rather down onto the street! (*Exit. Schigolch comes out.*)

SCHIGOLCH.—Blood!—Alva!—He's got to be put away

somewhere. Hop!—Or else our friends 'll get a shock from him—Alva! Alva!—He that isn't quite clear about it—! One thing or t'other; or it'll soon be too late! I'll give him legs! (*Strikes a match and sticks it into Alva's collar. . . .*) He will have his rest. But no one sleeps here.—(*Drags him by the head into Lulu's room. Returning, he tries to turn up the light.*) It'll be time for me, too, right soon now, or they'll get no more Christmas puddings down there in the tavern. God knows when she'll be coming back from her pleasure tour! (*Fixing an eye on Lulu's picture.*) She doesn't understand business! She can't live off love, because her life is love.—There she comes. I'll just talk straight to her once—(*Countess Geschwitz enters.*) . . . If you want to lodge with us to-night, kindly take a little care that nothing is stolen here.

GESCHWITZ. How dark it is here!

SCHIGOLCH. It gets much darker than this.—The doctor's already gone to rest.

GESCHWITZ. She sent me ahead.

SCHIGOLCH. That was sensible.—If anyone asks for me, I'm sitting downstairs in the pub.

GESCHWITZ. (*After he has gone.*) I will sit behind the door. I will look on at everything and not quiver an eye-lash. (*Sits on the broken chair.*) Men and women don't know themselves—they know not what they are. Only one who is neither man nor woman knows them. Every word they say is untrue, a lie. And they do not know it, for they are to-day so and to-morrow so, according as they have eaten, drunk, and loved, or not. Only the body remains for a time what it is, and only the children have reason. The men and women are like the animals: none knows what it does. When they are happiest they bewail themselves and groan, and in their deepest misery they rejoice over every tiny morsel. It is strange how hunger takes from men and women the strength to withstand misfortune. But when they have fed full they make this world a torture-chamber, they throw away their lives to satisfy a whim, a mood. Have there ever once been men and women to whom love brought happiness? And what is their happiness, save that they sleep better and can forget it all? My God, I thank thee that thou hast not made me as these. I am not man nor woman. My body has nothing common with their bodies. Have I a human soul? Tortured humanity has a little narrow heart; but I know I deserve nothing when I resign all, sacrifice all. . . . (*Lulu opens the door, and Dr. Hilti enters. Geschwitz, unnoticed, remains motionless by the door.*)

LULU. (*Gaily.*) Come right in! Come!—you'll stay with me all night?

DR. HILTI. (*His accent is very broad and flat.*) But I have no more than five shillings on me. I never take more than that when I go out.

LULU. That's enough, because it's you! You have such faithful eyes! Come, give me a kiss! (*Dr. Hilti begins to swear, in the broadest north-country vowels.*) Please, don't say that.

DR. HILTI. By the de'il, 'tis the first time I've e'er gone with a girrl! You can believe me. Mass, I hadn't thought it would be like this!

LULU. Are you married?

DR. HILTI. Heaven and Hail, why do you think I am married?—No, I'm a tutor; I read philosophy at the University. The truth is, I come of a very old country family. As a student, I got just two shillings pocket-money, and I could make better use of that than for girrls!

LULU. So you have never been with a woman?

DR. HILTI. Just so, yes! But I want it now. I got engaged this evening to a country-woman of mine. She's a governess here.

LULU. Is she pretty?

DR. HILTI. Yaw, she's got a hundred thousand.—I am very eager, as it seems to me . . .

LULU. (*Tossing back her hair.*) I am in luck! (*Takes the lamp.*) Well, if you please, Mr. Tutor? (*They go into her room. Geschwitz draws a small black revolver from her pocket and sets it to her forehead.*)

GESCHWITZ.—Come, come,—beloved! (*Dr. Hilti tears open the door again.*—)

DR. HILTI. (*Plunging in.*) Insane seraphs! Some one's lying in there!

LULU. (*Lamp in hand, holds him by the sleeve.*) Stay with me!

DR. HILTI. A dead man! A corpse!

LULU. Stay with me! Stay with me!

DR. HILTI. (*Tearing away.*) A corpse is lying in there! Horrors! Hail! Heaven!

LULU. Stay with me!

DR. HILTI. Where d's it go out? (*Sees Geschwitz.*) And there is the devil!

LULU. Please, stop, stay!

DR. HILTI. Devil, devilled devilry!—Oh, thou eternal— (*Exit.*)

LULU. (*Rushing after him.*) Stop! Stop!

GESCHWITZ. (*Alone, lets the revolver sink.*) Better, hang! If she sees me lie in my blood to-day she'll not weep a tear for me! I have always been to her but the docile tool that could be used for the heaviest labor. From the first day she has abhorred me from the depths of her soul.—Shall I not rather jump from the bridge? Which could be colder, the water or her heart? I would dream till I was drowned.—Better, hang!— —Stab?— Hm, there would be no use in that— —How often have I dreamt that she kissed me! But a minute more; an owl knocks there at the window, and I wake up.— —Better, hang! Not water; water is too clean for me. (*Starting up.*) There!—There! There it is!—Quick now, before she comes! (*Takes the plaid-straps from the wall, climbs on the chair, fastens them to a hook in the door-post, puts her head thru them, kicks the chair away, and falls to the ground.*) Accursed life!—Accursed life!—Could it be before me still??—Let me speak just once to thy heart, my angel! But thou art cold!—I am not to go yet! Perhaps I am even to have been happy once.—Listen to him, Lulu! I am not to go yet! (*She drags herself before Lulu's picture, sinks to her knees and folds her hands.*) My adoréd angel! My love! My star!—Have mercy upon me, pity me, pity me, pity me!

(*Lulu opens the door, and Jack enters—a thick-set man of elastic movements, with a pale face, inflamed eyes, arched and heavy brows, a drooping mustache, thin imperial and shaggy whiskers, and fiery red hands with gnawed nails. His eyes are fixed on the ground. He wears a dark overcoat and a little round felt hat. Entering, he notices Geschwitz.*)

JACK. Who is that?

LULU. That's my sister. She's crazy. I don't know how to get rid of her.

JACK. Your mouth looks beautiful.

LULU. It's my mother's.

JACK. Looks like it. How much do you want? I haven't got much money.

LULU. Won't you spend the night with me here?

JACK. No, haven't got the time. I must get home.

LULU. You can tell them at home to-morrow that you missed the last 'bus and spent the night with a friend.

JACK. How much do you want?

LULU. I'm not after lumps of gold, but, well, a little something.

JACK. (*Turning.*) Good night! Good night!

LULU. (*Holds him back.*) No, no! Stay, for God's sake!

JACK. (*Goes past Geschwitz and opens the cubicle.*) Why should I stay here till morning? Sounds suspicious! When I'm asleep they'll turn my pockets out.

LULU. No, I won't do that! No one will! Don't go away again for that! I beg you!

JACK. How much do you want?

LULU. Then give me the half of what I said!

JACK. No, that's too much. You don't seem to have been at this long?

LULU. To-day is the first time. (*She jerks back Geschwitz, on her knees still, half turned toward Jack, by the straps around her neck.*) Lie down and be quiet!

JACK. Let her alone! She isn't your sister. She is in love with you. (*Strokes Geschwitz's head like a dog's.*) Poor beast!

LULU. Why do you stare at me so all at once?

JACK. I got your measure by the way you walked. I said to myself: That girl must have a well-built body.

LULU. How can you see things like that?

JACK. I even saw that you had a pretty mouth. But I've only got a florin on me.

LULU. Well, what difference does that make! Just give that to me!

JACK. But you'll have to give me half back, so I can take the 'bus to-morrow morning.

LULU. I have nothing on me.

JACK. Just look, thoh. Hunt thru your pockets!— Well, what's that? Let's see it!

LULU. (*Showing him.*) That's all I have.

JACK. Give it to me!

LULU. I'll change it to-morrow, and then give you half.

JACK. No, give it all to me.

LULU. (*Giving it.*) In God's name! But now you come! (*Takes up the lamp.*)

JACK. We need no light. The moon's out.

LULU. (*Puts the lamp down.*) As you say. (*She falls on his neck.*) I won't harm you at all! I love you so! Don't let me beg you any longer!

JACK. Alright; I'm with you. (*Follows her into the cubby-hole. The lamp goes out. On the floor under the two sky-lights appear two vivid squares of moonlight. Everything in the room is clearly seen.*)

GESCHWITZ. (*As in a dream.*) This is the last evening I shall spend with these people. I'm going back to Germany. My mother'll send me the money. I'll go to a university. I must fight for woman's rights; study law. . . . (*Lulu shrieks, and tears open the door.*)

LULU. (*Barefoot, in chemise and petticoat, holding the door shut behind her.*) Help!

GESCHWITZ. (*Rushes to the door, draws her revolver, and pushing Lulu aside, aims it at the door. As Lulu again cries "Help!"*) Let go! (*Jack, bent double, tears open the door from inside, and runs a knife into Gesch-*

witz's body. She fires one shot, at the roof, and falls with suppressed crying, crumpling up. Jack tears her revolver from her and throws himself against the exit-door.)

JACK. God damn! I never saw a prettier mouth! (*Sweat drips from his hairy face. His hands are bloody. He pants, gasping violently, and stares at the floor with eyes popping out of his head. Lulu, trembling in every limb, looks wildly round. Suddenly she seizes the bottle, smashes it on the table, and with the broken neck in her hand rushes upon Jack. He swings up his right foot and throws her onto her back. Then he lifts her up.*)

LULU. No, no!—Mercy!—Murder!—Police! Police!

JACK. Be still. You'll never get away from me again. (*Carries her in.*)

LULU. (*Within, right.*) No!—No!—No!— —Ah! —Ah! . . .

(*After a pause, Jack re-enters. He puts the bowl on the table.*)

JACK. That *was* a piece of work! (*Washing his hands.*) I *am* a damned lucky chap! (*Looks round for a towel.*) Not even a towel, these folks here! Hell of a wretched hole! (*He dries his hands on Geschwitz's petticoat.*) This invert is safe enough from me! (*To her.*) It'll soon be all up with you, too. (*Exit.*)

GESCHWITZ. (*Alone.*) Lulu!—My angel!—Let me see thee once more! I am near thee—stay near thee—forever! (*Her elbows give way.*) O cursed—!! (*Dies.*)

CURTAIN.

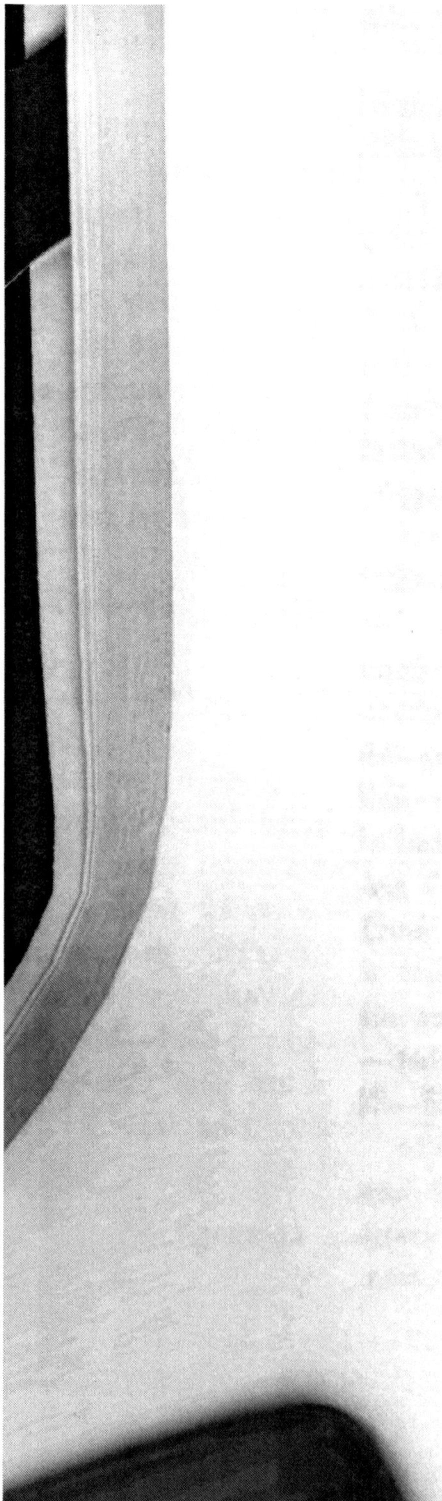

Lightning Source UK Ltd.
Milton Keynes UK
03 March 2011

168587UK00005B/31/P

9 781141 595648